# WRITE
# PUBLISH
# SELL

## *A Guide to Self-Publishing*

## Tonja Ayers

ISBN-13: 978-1522893288
ISBN-10: 1522893288

Cover design by Miles Dixon
Edited by Gloria Palmer
Proofread & Typeset by Gloria Palmer

Published by:
Emperial Publishing
P.O. Box 21402
Detroit, MI 48221
(313) 449-8543

Email: tonja@emperialpublishing.com
Website: www.emperialpublishing.com

First printing January 2016

# Table of Contents

# Chapter 1 - Getting Started:
# Know Your Genre

If you have always dreamed of being a writer, you can live your dreams by writing and publishing your own book. Self-publishing is the way many writers are choosing to get their book out to the public, and self-publishing today is not the same as it was years ago when you had to spend thousands of dollars to publish your book. You can self-publish a book for less than $500 when you choose a good self-publishing online service.

The first thing you need to do is "know" your genre. The one rule of writing is you should write what you know. If you have a specific genre you read, chances are this is what you will want to write about. Take a look at your interests and the type of books you read before you decide on your genre. Your book should never just be about making money; it should be about something for which you have a passion. There are many different genres available in both fiction and non-fiction. Before you start your book, have a plan of what it will be about and the genre it will fill.

You need to have a specific genre when you are writing a book so you will be able to market it properly. Some books will cross genre lines, such as paranormal and romance. Some books will fit neatly into a specific genre. It should be clear what the book is about to the reader so they will be interested in what you have written enough to buy the book. Most readers have types of books they like to read and tend to stick with one or two genres.

If you are writing a non-fiction book, there are also genres. You need to make your book stand out among the rest in a way that will set it apart from other books of the same genre. If you are writing an Italian cookbook, for example, how do you make it stand out from the other Italian cookbooks already on the market?

Once you find your genre and know what you are writing about, you should start to think of marketing your book. Make it something readers will choose when they see it in bookstores or online. This will set it apart from other books of its kind and entice readers to buy it. Many authors are finding they can make a career out of self-publishing their books and marketing them to the right audience.

After you have figured out what you are going to write about and what will make your book stand out among others, you can then start to outline your book. You should write down a synopsis of the book and the point you are trying to make. Good books carry a message; make sure your book has a message to the readers they can take away from the book at the end.

While you may like freeform writing, which is writing without doing any sort of outline, you should still have an idea of the ending of the book in your head. When you are writing fiction, characters tend to come to life as you write. Your ending may change as you rewrite; it is important to be flexible. The way you write depends on the type of person you are. If you prefer to have everything ironed out for your book, then you should do an outline that will tell you where you are going. This is like having a roadmap on a car trip.

There are some people, however, who do not want to use a roadmap on a trip; they just want to go. If this sounds like you, then just start writing and the ideas will start flowing in you. You can rework characters and plots as you move on in your book.

Everyone has a their own style when it comes to writing books. Overthinking the book and too much planning can bog you down and keep you from writing. Too little thought can keep your book from reaching a conclusion. It takes a lot of creativity as well as some structure in order to write a successful book that people will want to read.

Before you start writing your book, you should read books in the genre you are interested in so you get the feel for this type of writing. Reading is a good way to improve your writing skills and will give you a good idea of what you want to say in your book.

# Chapter 2 - Research Your Book

In order to write your book, you are going to have to do some research. Even if you are writing an autobiography, you still have to go back in your mind to research incidents that happened, and most likely look up dates and names. You want to do research to make your book seem more authentic and well-written. Nothing is worse than writing a book where you get facts, dates, and/or other information wrong.

Research different types of books that have been successful in the genre you have chosen for your book. When you are performing research, you can use your local library as well as the internet. If you are writing fiction, you will need to do even more research. For example, if you are writing a murder mystery, you need to know police procedures as well as how murderers are caught. You can discover this information through your research by taking a look at the books at the local library. Some authors go as far to take a class in something they want to learn about at a community college so they can be better prepared for their book.

You do not want to get bogged down with research, however. Many writers enjoy research so much that they neglect to write their book. This is not what you want to do. You want to research your book so you have the right information, but not write a thesis. Too much research can stunt the creative flow of your book. One way to research what you are writing is to do the research after you have finished the first draft of your book; another way is to research as you are writing. The internet makes it easier to do research now more than ever, and you can get most—if not all—the information online you need to research your book.

It is a good idea to research the characters in your book, even if they are fictional. Discover some information about the personality traits of people. A good writer is very much in tune with the human psyche and the way people think. In fact, if you want to get in touch with the characters you create, you can do so by learning a bit of psychology. Creative writers are often advised to take this class so they can get in touch with the way people think and react to certain situations. By learning how others think, you will be able to bring more to the book than your own perception of how to react in a certain situation. This will also help you with dialogue as well. Realistic dialogue is very important when writing a book. If you understand how and why people react a certain way and speak in certain terms, you can give your characters more depth.

In addition to researching your characters and the plot of your book, you should also make sure you do some research on what makes a good book. You can take a writing course to learn how to write a good book or even join a writing group. The more input you get from other writers and the more information you share, the better your book will be.

There are conferences you can attend for writers as well as workshops. You can make these all part of your writing research as an addition to researching your book. You should also research the components that make up a good book.

A good book has the following:

* Three-dimensional, believable characters
* A conflict
* A climax
* A resolution to the conflict

You should have some sort of conflict in the book that is presented right from the start. Many authors believe the conflict must be resolved by the ending of the book. This does not mean your book has to have a happy ending, but some think you shouldn't leave anything hanging that remains unsolved. However, I beg to differ. Isn't that how sequels are created?

Everyone's writing style is unique and there is nothing wrong with going outside the box. The climax is very important as well and you want to pen your book so it reaches a climax that builds up throughout the book. Another thing you need to determine is which point of view you want to use to write the book. You can choose first-person narrative, which is an easier style to write, but is limited to the thoughts and actions of the main character, or narrator of the story. You can write first-person observant, which tells the story from the point of view of another character who is observing the action. You can choose third person and still write from the point of view of the main protagonist. When you are writing in the third person, you can also delve into the point of view from other characters in the book. Of all the styles of writing, third-person omniscient, which sees into the heads of all the characters, is the most difficult to write. Take a look at books you like to read and see which writing style best fits your book. The point of view you write from can make or break your book.

In addition to point of view, you also need to decide if you are writing in the past or present tense. Most books are written in the past tense. Writing in the present tense is more difficult, but lends more action to the book.

Do your research by studying other books and your own writing style to see which point of view and tense you wish to use in your book. First-person narrative, which is also called prose writing, is the easiest, but has limitations. Third-person omniscient is the most difficult, but opens up the thoughts and feelings of other characters in the book. This type of research should be done before you start your book, but can be changed if you find it isn't working for you and how you want to tell a story.

# Chapter 3 - Fiction Or Non-Fiction?

Most people equate writing a book only with writing a novel, which is a fiction story. This is not the case when it comes to writing, especially writing today. There is a very big market for non-fiction books as well. Cookbooks, how-to books, motivational books, and biographies are all examples of non-fiction books that sell very well and are often self-published. In order to get a book published by mainstream press that is non-fiction, you have to have a well-known name or a very unique idea. You also need to be extremely lucky as there is major competition in the mainstream press for authors, especially unknown authors.

Fiction books tell a story, and have a conflict and a resolution. Non-fiction books do not follow along the same lines. For example, there is no conflict in writing a cookbook. There is a market for all types of non-fiction books, and this can be an easy way to publish your first book.

If you are writing a non-fiction book, you need to do heavy research and be very well-versed on the topic which you are writing. You should also have an angle to your book that makes it unique from others. Motivational books are a good example, as there are many of them on the market right now. What can you do to make your book different?

One example of a different type of motivational book is the *Laws of Attraction* series. This took an old idea, put a new spin on it, and created a series of very successful motivational books.

Biographies do not always have to be about famous people. You can write a biography about anyone who has led an extraordinary life or influenced many people. Cleverly-crafted biographies about ordinary people who have proved to be inspirational to others are very popular today. You need to have the permission of the person about whom you are writing or their estate in order to write a good biography.

There have been unauthorized biographies that have made a sensation, but still required the person to do a lot of research on the subject, although they were not given the same amount of respect as biographies that were done with the consent of the person the biography was about. You also risk a lawsuit, such as was the case with Kitty Kelley, who wrote a slew of unauthorized biographies about famous people and found herself being sued by the late Frank Sinatra.

Cookbooks are very popular, especially when it comes to self-published books. Your cookbook needs to have something different, a unique angle, in order to sell. Why would anyone buy your book of French recipes when they can get the same from Julia Child's cookbooks? One way to make yours unique is to add a bit of the French countryside and perhaps some fiction or historical information in with the recipes. This will prove to be entertaining to the reader as well as informational.

If you are going to write a novel, you have to prepare as outlined in the previous chapter. Your novel should be of a genre that you like, and most of all, something you would buy yourself if it was available in the bookstore. You can put a lot of creative passion in your novel and turn it into something that will stand out. Many people self-publish novels because the competition is so great to get a novel published by an unknown author in the mainstream press.

When you self-publish, you do not need an agent to help you get your book to a publisher. The catch-22 if you decide not to self-publish is some mainstream press companies will only work with an agent. Working with an agent is a good idea if you are trying to publish in this way. Most agents, however, only want to work with a person who has a previously-published novel. Needless to say, this makes it very difficult for someone to break into the mainstream press with their first book.

Even if you did manage to get a book published by a publisher, you still might have to market the book on your own. If you self-publish, you can do the same type of marketing. Because so many people today buy books online, self-publishing is quickly becoming the publishing form of choice for authors writing fiction and non-fiction.

Whether you write fiction or non-fiction is up to you. If you have a lot of creative energy and can make up plots and characters in your head, fiction writing may be for you. If you consider yourself an expert in a certain field, non-fiction writing is for you. You can use self-publishing for both non-fiction and fiction books.

# Chapter 4 - Completing the First Draft

Once you have decided on the book you want to write, you should start on your first draft. This may change drastically by the time the book is completed, although chances are you will keep some of the information in the final book that you have in your first draft.

Everyone writes in a different way. There are those who rewrite as they go along in a book, and those who complete the first draft before attempting any rewriting. It is best to write the first draft and get it all on paper, or computer, before you start any rewriting. This can allow you to see the direction your book has taken and how it looks. You should not get discouraged if your first draft is less than magnificent; this is only your first draft.

Many writers of fiction like to get that first draft finished before they start any research into the book. Having the first draft completed does not mean you have completed your book, but you have completed a rough draft of your book. The average novel is between sixty thousand and eighty thousand words, although the rough draft may be less.

In some cases, writers will sketch out a first draft that is mostly narrative. It contains only sparse dialogue, to be put in later when rewriting. If you are writing a fiction book, this is a good way to get the book down on paper, see if the plot makes sense, and make sure you present a conflict and a resolution to the conflict.

There are two types of conflict that can be contained in your book. These are either internal conflicts or external conflicts. Internal conflicts are those that take place in the minds of the characters of the book. They can be due to their perception of the world or their perception about another individual. External conflicts are those that are caused by outside influences. Misunderstandings or third parties getting in the way are examples of external conflicts that arise in fiction books.

A good way to figure out the conflict in the book is to present the reader with a question that will be answered at the end of the book. This type of conflict is often used in murder mysteries. The reader does not know who committed the murder until the climax of the book, after which the conflict has been resolved. A good book presents not only external conflicts, but internal conflicts as well. It also may present a series of conflicts in the book that come together to be resolved by the time the book ends. It is important to create conflict in a fiction book that will keep the reader reading and wanting to see a resolution in the end.

A good book also makes a point. There can be symbolism in the book as well as a subtle message that the book is trying to get across to the reader. While not all books contain these variables, they are found in some of the great novels.

Another factor you want to add into your fiction book is foreshadowing. This should be presented throughout the book, but especially in the beginning. This gets the reader hooked early on so they want to continue to see what happens in the book. They will be anxious to get to the end of the book to discover the reason for the foreshadowing. Foreshadowing implies that something will happen to change the world of the characters early in the book. This intrigues the reader and makes them want to continue reading.

The first paragraph of your book is probably the most important part of the book. This is the paragraph that will either hook or bore the reader. One problem many authors have when it comes to writing a book that is interesting is a slow start. This fails to pull the reader in and keep them interested in reading the book. Including foreshadowing in the first paragraph is a good idea. Another thing you can do to make your book more interesting to the reader is to start in the middle. Instead of starting the book from the beginning, you can start in the middle of the story and then take the reader back, through the use of dialogue and narrative to the beginning of the story, to fill them in on the history.

Another option is telling the story backwards, starting from the ending. One of the hottest shows on television now is *How to Get Away with Murder*, which started its first episode of the season with the ending. The remaining episodes narrated what happened to cause the events showcased in the initial episode

The climax of the book is also important in a fiction book. The plot should build up to the climax. You may have several anti-climaxes as well in the book as other conflicts are resolved. The main conflict in the book must be resolved by the end of the book.

Do not make the mistake of introducing characters at the end of the book who figure heavily into the resolution of the plot. For example, if you are writing a murder mystery, you need to have the murderer figure in the book early on. Some writers will make it look as if someone is obviously guilty, but the culprit is someone the reader does not suspect. You want to keep your reader hungry for more as they get to the end of the book`.

While the first paragraph, climax, and conflict resolution are integral parts of the book, do not fill your book with fluff. Each character in the book should figure somewhat in the plot. Each sentence in the book should move the plot forward. This does not often happen in the first draft of the book, but will happen as you continue with rewrites. Remember that any book, even a non-fiction book, does not appear in print the way it came out of your head. You have to be prepared for rewriting.

# Chapter 5 - Rewriting

Ernest Hemingway suggested rewriting a book thirty times before it is ready for publication. His reasoning was that, each time the writer goes over the book for rewriting, they have a better understanding into the minds of the characters. Of course I'm not suggesting thirty rewrites, but with careful preparation, fewer rewrites will be required. Prepare a character description sheet. Write detailed descriptions such as hair length, eye color, and body type; also include habits or hobbies such as reading, smoking, or drinking. The more descriptive you are, the easier it will be when describing your characters for your audience. The more you get to know your characters, the more you will be able to write convincing dialogue and a narrative that will suit them.

One important thing to remember when you are rewriting is not to be afraid of making major changes in your book. If something is not working and doesn't feel right, change it. It is important not to get married to your book. While you'll have a natural passion for the book, you should also be open-minded enough to realize if something isn't working in your plot, you have to fix it.

The best way to start rewriting is to read through your first draft. You can then note inconsistencies and other plot problems that occur with the first draft. You should begin your rewriting from the beginning of the book to the end, especially if you are writing a fiction book that will have character development. Even if you are writing non-fiction, you still want to rewrite your book to tighten it up.

Try not to use a passive voice when you are writing. This is when you put in words like "would have" and "was". Try to use more action words in your book; otherwise it may tend to get sluggish. Also, go over the dialogue and make sure it seems natural. You want to look at dialogue as well as consistency when you are rewriting your book.

Do not be surprised if your book has an ending other than what you had imagined. Many times, writers grow to like some characters and dislike others. The creative process takes on a mind of its own when an author is writing a book. This often means inconsistencies in the book and with the characters.

Each time you rewrite the book, you are making it a better story. You have a better feel for the characters in the story with each writing and they become more lifelike to you—so much so that you can figure out what they like for breakfast or what is their favorite color. By including personality traits in the book that are distinguishable to each character, you make them more lifelike for the reader.

The more you get to know the characters in your book, the more lifelike they will seem to the reader. You want to get away from flat characters and breathe some life into them. The only way you can do this when writing a fiction book is to get to know them. This is naturally more difficult to do with fiction than non-fiction because the characters are a figment of your imagination. You have to want to make your imagination come to life on paper when you write your book.

Get rid of unnecessary dialogue that slows down the process of your book as well as unnecessary descriptions. The best books are those that continue to move the plot forward and have meaning in every sentence.

Do not mistake rewriting as checking for grammar or spelling. This will be done when you are proofreading your book, although you should naturally make any corrections when you see them. Proofreading is very different than rewriting and will be discussed shortly.

One thing you may want to do to make your rewriting easier is to give yourself a rest between the rewrites. This allows you to look at the book with fresh eyes and get a fresh start reading it. If you have a friend or trusted person to whom you can give the book, give it to them for a critique. They may be able to see glaring errors in the plot you may overlook. While you are close to your book, you may also be too close. It is helpful to have a second pair of eyes read the book after you have rewritten it to sufficiency.

You cannot rewrite a book too much, but there does have to be a point where you say you are satisfied with the story and what it conveys. After you have completed your book and feel it is publication worthy, you are ready for a grammar check.

Go through your book and look for grammatical errors. There are some instances when grammatical rules are broken, especially when it comes to dialogue. Otherwise, you want to make sure you have used proper grammar in your book. If you have a grammar check on your word processing program, use it. You should also use spellcheck as well. However, never depend on the spellchecker and grammar checker to do your proofreading for you. When you have finished your book, it is time for proofreading.

# Chapter 6 - Proofreading Your Book

Take the book and print it out on paper for proofreading. Then, starting with the last page and moving backward, use a ruler to look at each line in the book. This is a tedious process and one for which you can pay a freelance proof-reader. You are looking for spelling mistakes as well as mistakes in punctuation. When we read, our eyes naturally gloss over words we are familiar with and often do not see they are misspelled. This is why it is important to take your time and proofread your book from finish to start. By going up one line at a time, you will not be reading, but looking for errors that your eyes will ignore if you simply read the book.

You can hire a professional proof-reader for this purpose. They will go through the book the way that suits them and deliver you a product that has changes. They will put proofreading marks on your paper of which you should be familiar. They will not make the changes for you, but will mark where you should make the changes.

It is vital that you proofread your book or have someone else do it for you. If you have a book published by the mainstream press, this service is done for you. If you are self-publishing, however, you do not have this luxury. There are many self-publishing companies online that offer proofreading services for a price for their clients. These services usually charge more than freelancers who you can also find online.

One place you can find proof-readers who will go over your book for you is *Elance.com*. This site has a multitude of freelancers offering their services. Be sure to check out their profiles as well as reviews from other clients before you ask them to proofread your material. You can put your project on the site for bidding. Be sure you do not automatically go for the lowest bid. Check out experience and customer satisfaction, which signify that the proof-reader knows what he or she is doing.

Proofreading a book is not like editing a book. Copyediting is a completely different process altogether. You can choose to copyedit your own book or have the company that publishes the book for you do the job. We will discuss editing for your self-published book later.

If you decide to proofread your book yourself, take your time and do it correctly. Do not rush through this process, as an array of misspelled words in your book will make it look less than professional to the reader. You want your book to be as professional as possible so the reader does not get turned off. You can keep it free from typos, punctuation, and spelling errors by doing careful proofreading or hiring someone to do the job for you.

Even if you have someone who is not a professional proof-reader take a look at your book, this is a fresh pair of eyes, so they can see errors where you cannot. Remember, you have a very strong connection to your book that others do not. You have most likely read it over and over again. Having someone who has not looked at the book take a look for errors can help you out tremendously. Most professional proof-readers will charge by the page. This may be an investment you will want to make if you are serious about making sure your book is error free.

Remember that even books published by the mainstream press have errors. Having one error in the book is not the end of the world. Having a boatload of errors, however, can make your book look shoddy and not well put together.

# Chapter 7 - Editing For Your Self-Published Book

Editing your book is different than proofreading. You need to pay attention to style as well as grammar when you are copyediting. It pays to have good grammatical skills and have a certain style you use for your book when you are considering your own editing.

Most of the self-publishing sites offer copyediting services for an extra charge. This can help you over awkward phrases you may not notice in your book as well as other grammatical problems. You may say something in a way you do not mean when you are writing a book. It may make sense to you, but not to others. A copyeditor will read your book with a fresh pair of eyes and pick out errors. They will also pay attention to style and pick out any spelling errors they see.

Copyediting for a book will also help you tighten up your book. In some cases, it will eliminate repetitive sentences or words that bog down your book. Copyediting is not like regular editing, which will take a good look at your book to see if it makes sense. An editor will usually make suggestions for broader changes than a copyeditor.

It is a good idea to pay someone to edit your book. You should at least hire someone to copyedit the book. You can go to Elance, contact me for an editor referral, or you can pay for the editing from a self-publishing company. The cost varies but can be the best money you spend when you self-publishing a book. An editor can make sure that everything in the book makes sense and is written in the same style.

Writers often have a habit of switching styles when they are writing. Most writers have a creative streak that causes them to write. It can be difficult for them to edit their own work just as it can be difficult for them to proofread their own work. Again, spending the money for editing is one of the best investments a writer can make.

# Chapter 8 – Copyrighting Your Book

Many authors ask if they should copyright their books. Yes, you should. Even though the work is automatically protected just by writing it, it doesn't mean you'll be able to prove it. Look at a copyright registration as a life insurance policy for your book.

The following are benefits of copyright registration:

1.  Copyright registration establishes a public record of your copyright.

2.  You cannot sue anyone for copyright infringement if your book isn't registered with the Copyright Office.

3.  No award for statutory damages or attorney fees will be made for any infringement of a copyright in an unpublished book which occurs prior to registration of the copyright. The same holds true for published books, unless the registration is made within three months after the first publication.

4.  If the registration of your book is done within five years from its creation, it is considered "prima facie" evidence in court. Prima facie evidence means, if you ever went to court, the registration of your copyright would be sufficient evidence of your ownership of the copyrighted material. The only way for another party to win would be for them to present evidence showing:

    a.  They had a pre-existing copyright claim to the work.

    b.  You permitted them to use your work.

    c.  You didn't actually create the work.

d.    You stole it from them.

U.S. Copyright registrations are recognized by the courts in one hundred sixty-seven other countries!

The easiest way to copyright is to file the registration online directly with the U.S. Copyright Office at *www.copyright.gov/eco/*. You are required to file the "best edition" of your work. So, if you don't want to have to send two final, printed copies of your book, upload the final pdf before it goes off to the printer.

If you file your copyright online with the U.S. Copyright Office, the fee is $35. If you mail in your work and the registration forms, the fee is $45. Many self-publishing companies include copyright registration as part of their packages or offer it as a stand-alone service. You should never pay more than $150 for this service (which should include the Copyright Office filing fee of $35 for online filings and $45 for paper filings). For the extra few dollars, this service is worthwhile.

The turnaround time by the Copyright Office is six months for electronic filings and up to twenty-two months for paper filings; however, the effective filing date of the registration is the date it arrives at the U.S. Copyright Office, not when they process it. Also, under certain circumstances (like pending litigation), the U.S. Copyright Office will expedite the filing of a copyright. However, the fee for this is $760.

# Chapter 9 - Finding a Self-Publisher Online

Years ago, if someone wanted to get a book self-published, they had to pay thousands of dollars. A press would publish the book for the individual and give them a certain number of copies. All of the copies, plus the fees involved in setting the press and printing, were paid for by the author of the self-published book. Those who sought to have their books self-published were not thought to be good authors. The name used for self-publishing then was "vanity press". It was thought that those who got their books published this way just had the money, not the talent, needed to be a writer.

With the change in technology, and how people send and receive data nowadays, that belief is so far from the truth. Many talented authors have decided to eliminate the middle man, self-fund their own projects, and build a name for themselves. Mainstream press takes very few authors and is so competitive, self-publishing is a way for writers to have their voices heard.

There have been stories of those who submitted, just for fun, a first chapter and query letter of a great novel to publishers to see if they would actually read them. They were returned with standard rejection letters. Many publishing houses will not take writers who are not represented by agents. This makes it very difficult for someone to get their book published, as most agents who deal with these publishers only deal with established authors.

Some authors decide to publish their books using small-press publishers. These publishers don't charge a writer for printing their book, but also don't have the clout to get the book reviewed in the New York Times. The writer has to do all the marketing for the book and only receives a small portion of the royalties.

Needless to say, it makes more sense for a new writer to self-publish their book and market it themselves. They can use modern self-publishers who print-to-order and do not charge an enormous fee for publishing a book. The books are given ISBN numbers and are listed on places like Amazon, where most people today are buying their books. The author can get their book in a bookstore as long as it has an ISBN. There are many ways for a self-published author to market their book.

Since you will most likely do the marketing anyway when you get your book published, you might as well self-publish your book with a publisher who does print-to-order publishing. This way, you get a higher percentage of the profits and the book can be listed online for those who are interested in buying it. Self-publishing is the way many writers today, even those who have been published by small-press, are deciding to publish their book.

Two places you can go online to self-publish your book are Lulu.com and CreateSpace.com. Both of these are well known with self-publishers and print-to-order. You can acquire other services from these companies as well, including formatting your book.

Lulu gives you tools to format your book yourself. You need to submit a PDF to Lulu in order for them to be able to print your book. If you have a PDF converter or Adobe, you can format your own book through this company. They give you a choice of hard cover or soft cover, as well as different sizes of the book. Pricing for printing varies on the size, page count, and quantity of your book. The books are listed on the Lulu website and you can also have them listed on Amazon. This is a good option for those who have little money, have some computer skills, and are able to format the book on their own. You can also pay them to format the book for you.

CreateSpace.com has many benefits, such as creating your own estore. One of the biggest benefits is no minimum order when ordering books. You can order one book or a thousand books; it's up to you. It is also less money than other self-publishing sites, and your book can be listed on Amazon as well as other distribution channels.

Both of these sites print-to-order, which means you do not have to order a bunch of books. They will print a book when a customer orders it and ship it out for you. You get paid a percentage of the books you sell, which is a higher percentage than what you would get with a mainstream publisher and much more than you can get with small-press publishing. If you take the time to market your book, which you can do, you can end up making a lot more money and getting your book out to readers.

Take a look online and find a website that will offer you print-to-order books. You will get a percentage of the books you buy for yourself as well. You can purchase the books yourself and get them in bookstores as well as book fairs and exhibits for self-published writers. Bookstores will take a book as long as there is an ISBN on it. The book publisher will also include a barcode on the book.

According to *Forbes* magazine, Mark Dawson, a self-published author receives $450,000 annually from Amazon. Dawson has published a successful crime-thriller series. The tactics he employed to promote his series aren't game-changing, or even particularly clever, but the scale in which he implemented them is what made the difference. To date, he has sold over three hundred thousand copies of his series about an assassin called John Milton. Dawson says he pocketed "six figures" last year, and he's on course to make much more this year.

There are many more options open now than ever before for those who want to self-publish their books. Because of internet and computer technologies, it is easy for any writer to get their book published through self-publishing. An increasing number of writers are seeking out self-publishing to make money and get their books out to the readers who are eager to read them.

# Chapter 10 - Printing Your Own Book

Another way to get your book self-published is to print your book yourself. You can do this at a number of different places, although you have to format your book yourself as well as prepare it for the printing press.

Online printers will print up your book. You can purchase an ISBN number yourself by going to the site at *isbn.org*. You need a number for each of your books. You will receive a barcode to put on your book that you print yourself.

Printing your own book is a lot of work. It takes some knowledge in how to format the book as well as design the cover. You can use an offline printer as well as an online printer. You just have to get everything ready for printing, including the cover. The cover will be made of a thicker paper and can be glossy or matte. The cover is a very important part of the book, so it is a good idea to hire an experienced graphic artist to design the cover if you are planning on printing the book yourself and want your cover to look professional.

In order to get an ISBN, you have to set up a publishing company of your own. You can do this easily enough, then apply for the ISBN. It can be costly to pay for these numbers on a single basis, which is why it often pays to have the self-publishing company print the book for you and get the ISBN. Because they order more of them, they receive them at a lower price. If you are planning on printing more than one book, you can order a series of ten ISBN numbers and receive a discounted price. Self-publishing companies order these by the hundreds, which is why they can provide a number for customers included in their printing price.

You also have to also figure that you will have to do your own editing and proofreading when you are printing up your own book. This can be very time consuming, which is why many writers prefer to pay the money to a self-publishing company.

Printing your own book may work if you have a small literary magazine you put out. It can work if you just want to distribute books personally and sell them. It can work if you are planning to sell your book on your own. You have to remember that, even with an ISBN, a book store may be reluctant to put a book on their shelves that does not look as if it has been professionally printed. Decide how you want to sell your book and where, then decide how you wish to have it printed.

# Chapter 11 - Your Book Is Printed; Now What?

After you have your book printed and ready to go, what do you do? You do the same thing that you would do if your book was published by a mainstream publishing company—promote it!

There are many ways you can promote your book, both online and off. One thing you will want to do is to promote your book by getting some positive reviews on Amazon. If you have your book listed on Amazon, you can get reviews for the book from a book reviewing service. You can send them a disk with the book on it in pdf format, and have people read it and give it a good review. The more reviews it gets, the more it will rise in Amazon.

Don't be afraid to ask customers to leave a review when you're selling your book hand-to-hand. Friends and family are easily accessible reviewers as well. Place the book reviews you have received on various book review websites online. There are many sites where you can place reviews of your book. You can also put a link to the book's website on these sites.

You should have a website as a teaser for your book. When you have a website, you can sell books directly from the site or you can send the buyers to Amazon. You can become an affiliate of Amazon and get paid a commission on all your sales. You should also have a post office box or business address to use when people order your book by mail. In addition, you can also direct them to the self-publishing company where they can find the book. You can then market your website using strategies used to market any website.

If your book is non-fiction, you'll want to write articles and place them in article hubs on the internet. Article hubs will allow you to place free articles online. Do a Google keyword analytics to see which are the right keywords for your book. You can write articles with these keywords and place them on the different sites with a backlink to your site.

In addition to promoting your book online through the use of the website and book reviews, you can also join writing groups for self-published writers. There are many sites for self-published writers you can take advantage of to promote your book. You should also look into local libraries that often have groups for self-published authors. There are often book fairs for self-published authors as well.

You can send your book to different newspapers and local magazines that review books. Bear in mind, papers like the *New York Times* and magazines like the *New Yorker* have many books that people want them to review. You have a better chance of getting your book reviewed by magazines that are genre-related to the book you have written.

Small, independent bookstores will feature your book, especially if they are local bookstores. You should take your book there, buying up several copies of the book for selling, then have a book signing. Most bookstores are more than happy to have local authors' visit and sign books. This can be advertised through flyers and in the bookstore itself. This brings business to the store as well as gets you recognition.

If you have a small local newspaper, you can use them for publicity for your book. Small, hometown newspapers are an ideal way to spread the word about your book.

You can also take your book to gift shops that will sell it on consignment. Be sure to match the type of marketing you do to the venue to get the word about your book out there. Leave no stone unturned when you are marketing your book.

# Chapter 12 - Online Marketing to Sell Your Book

The best way to sell your book is online. Your first venue will usually be the self-publishing company that prints your book. They not only print books but also sell books written by their authors. You can depend on many sales from a self-published book from the website.

Be sure to tell family and friends you have published a book and encourage them to buy it online rather than from you. Most websites rate books on the sales, so you want to make sure sales go through the website. Also ask them to share their purchase on their social media websites.

Most of the online print-to-order sites will list the books on Amazon. Amazon is the biggest seller of books in the world. Getting your book listed on Amazon is the same as having it on a shelf in a bookstore. But remember, if no one knows you have a book out, they won't find it unless they stumble upon it.

Use social networking sites like Facebook, Instagram, LinkedIn, YouTube, and Twitter to get the word out about your book. You can also place links to the book page on various forums. You do want to get a website so you can spread the word about your book. Developing your own website and getting a host is neither difficult nor expensive. You can have a website and host for your book very inexpensively.

You cannot afford to ignore the power of online marketing when it comes to selling your book. The fact is today many books are sold online; in fact, the vast majority of people sell their books online. You want to be sure you do your best to market your book as much as possible on the internet.

You will find you will get more sales from online sales than you will from bookstore sales. While it is important to get as much exposure as possible for your book, you need to concentrate heavily on online exposure for your book so you can make sales.

# Chapter 13 - Offline Marketing
# To Sell Your Book

You will want to get as much exposure offline as well. We have already talked about groups you can join and getting your books in bookstores to do book signings.

Book signings are the best way for you to get exposure with your book. You can do them in any local bookstore. They will be glad to have you. You can bring your books to the bookstore to sell them.

Larger bookstores, such as Barnes & Noble, will want you to go through the main office in order to have your book stocked on their shelves. These stores will want to see a copy of your book before they place an order. This can be time consuming for you, but is well worth the try.

You are better off approaching the manager of a bookstore and offering them the books on a consignment basis. They will let you do a book signing and you can bring your own books, but you will have to give a commission to the store.

You can use a book distributor to distribute your book to local bookstores to get them on the shelves. This may be easier than going through the corporate route. You will have to buy the books from the publishing company in order to get them to the distributor. The distributor will then work to get the books to the major bookstores.

Again, this is a tough sell. Best sellers from major presses have more shelf space in bookstores as well as the prominent shelf spaces. Just like in the supermarket, the biggest distributors have the most attractive shelf spaces. If you think you will see your book on the center shelf at a major bookstore, think again. If they take your book, it will be in the shelves. This is why you need to promote the book with book signings. You should still do what you need to do to get the book at the bookstore.

There are plenty of local, independent bookstores available. They are much more receptive to local authors and will eagerly take your book on a consignment basis. They will be happy to have you come in to do a book signing. Take a look at independent bookstores in your area.

Make sure you join an offline group of self-publishers and take advantage of book fairs that are specifically for self-publishing authors. You can also make up bookmarks for your book to be handed out at these fairs. The bookmarks should have information about the book as well as where readers can find it.

You have to do some legwork to get your book out there to the public. You need to be sure to do as much as you can to get the book's information out there. The more you continue to promote your book, the more interest it will generate.

When you go through the time and work of putting all of your creative talent into a book, you want to do what you can to make sure the book is read. Most good writers are not as much interested in the money for the book as they are in the book being read by others.

Having your book read and enjoyed by other people is the most gratifying thing a writer can experience. Working hard to complete and print your book then have having others enjoy your writing is one of the best things a writer can experience.

If you have been considering writing a book but are not sure if you can get a publisher, you should consider self-publishing. Instead of trying to get an agent and a publisher to look at your book, then only give you a small percentage of the profit, you can easily self-publish your own book and have others read it.

Go online and take a look at the following sites:

*www.lulu.com*
*www.createspace.com*

These are two of the most popular sites online for self-publishing. Take a look at their frequently-asked questions and rates to see which is right for you. Then get started writing and making your dream come true!

Good luck and I wish you much success with your writing endeavors. For questions or comments, please feel free to contact me at www.TonjaAyers.com.

www.ingramcontent.com/pod-product-compliance
Lightning Source LLC
Chambersburg PA
CBHW071259280526
45788CB00004B/1777